D0373346

Woman of Wisdom

Trust in the Lord with all your heart and lean not on your own understanding; in all your ways acknowledge him, and he will make your paths straight.

Proverbs 3:5 6

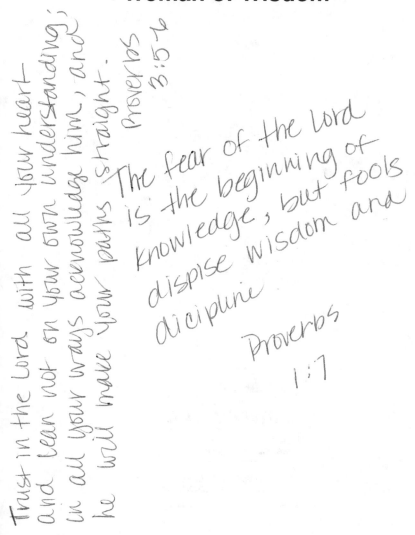

The fear of the Lord is the beginning of knowledge, but fools dispise wisdom and dicipline

Proverbs 1:7

Discovery House
PUBLISHERS
BOX 3566 · GRAND RAPIDS, MI 49501

PUBLISHING BOOKS THAT FEED
THE SOUL WITH THE WORD OF GOD.

Woman of Wisdom

Lessons for Living
from the Book of Proverbs

Myrna Alexander

Woman of Wisdom:
Lessons for Living from the Book of Proverbs

Copyright © 1992 by Myrna Alexander

Unless otherwise indicated, Scripture is taken from the
HOLY BIBLE, NEW INTERNATIONAL VERSION.
Copyright © 1973, 1978, 1984 International Bible Society.
Used by permission of Zondervan Bible Publishers.

Library of Congress Cataloging-in-Publication Data

Alexander, Myrna.
Woman of wisdom : lessons for living from the book of Proverbs /
Myrna Alexander
p. cm.

ISBN 0-929239-56-3

1. Bible. O.T. Proverbs—Study and teaching. I. Title.
BS1467.A44 1992   223'.70076—dc20   92-5466
CIP

Discovery House Publishers is affiliated with Radio Bible Class,
Grand Rapids, Michigan

Discovery House books are distributed to the trade by
Thomas Nelson Publishers, Nashville, Tennessee 37214.

All rights reserved.

Printed in the United States of America

92 93 94 95 96 / CHG / 10 9 8 7 6 5 4 3 2

To my parents
and my husband's parents
who taught their children
to revere God.

Contents

Acknowledgments

No work for God is achieved single-handedly. His work is accomplished when the parts of Christ's body work together (1 Corinthians 12:7). It's then that the clearest statement concerning God is best made. *A Woman of Wisdom* illustrates this principle for it is the result of God at work in His people.

I am grateful to Dr. Bruce Waltke for his series on "Wisdom Literature" delivered at Western Conservative Baptist Seminary. These lectures first challenged me to view Proverbs as a whole. Dr. Waltke's words created within me a desire to know God through Proverbs.

I am also thankful for the women who originally studied this material in our weekly Women's Bible Study both in Grace Community Church, Gresham, Oregon, and Vienna International Chapel, Vienna, Austria. Their interaction proved invaluable to me.

I'm very appreciative of Carolyn Potsch, who reviewed each lesson and offered many wise insights.

I am deeply grateful for the dedication and skill of my typist and friend, Sylvia Jones, without whom these lessons would never have arrived at the publisher.

Finally, I am continually thankful for my husband's biblical scholarship, wise counsel, and constant encouragement in the study of the Scriptures. And I am so grateful for the specific prayer support of my family, friends, and church family.

Preface

God describes a truly excellent woman as one who "opens her mouth in wisdom and the law of kindness is on her tongue" (Proverbs 31:26). Most women, and I am certainly one, would love to see this caption written over their names. But how is it possible? What makes it happen? The book of Proverbs involves itself with this question, for its purpose is to enable one to know wisdom and understanding (Proverbs 1).

Proverbs shows us not only the crucial starting place for true wisdom, but also the outworking of wisdom in everyday life. Why is wisdom so important? It is the way to live life with skill, like an accomplished craftsman who creates something of lasting value—in this case eternal!

Our brief-as-grass hours are filled with decisions over the details of living. Proverbs gives explicit counsel about how life should be lived for our own good, as well as that of others. This book makes us aware that God will be glorified through even our smallest action. Thus, Proverbs lifts everyday life once and for all out of what man calls ordinary into the extraordinary of permanent significance.

In Proverbs God makes it plain that wisdom is available to any woman who makes the decision of faith to meet God's prerequisites, as revealed in Proverbs 2:1–4. Wisdom's invitation is clear and encouraging, " 'Let all who are simple come in here!' she says to those who lack judgment. 'Come, eat my food and drink the wine I have mixed. Leave your simple ways and you will live; walk in the way of understanding' " (Proverbs 9:4–6). Do this and God promises that "wisdom will enter your heart."

What foolishness then if you and I would not make our ears attentive and incline our hearts to receive and understand the truths in this book!

How To Use This Bible Study

A Woman of Wisdom was originally written for women who wanted to study the Bible together as a group after having studied a passage on their own during the week. I believe individual study is the key to a group Bible study whose goal is to see lives changed. Growth and encouragement took place in our group because we came together prepared to interact with God's principles.

Effective study of the Bible involves commitment. Consequently this study guide requires consistent and serious study. The result of the work is fruitful and life-changing group discussions.

The lessons are intended to be done on a regular basis: one discovery section per day, one lesson per week. There is, however, room for flexibility according to the needs of the individual or group using the material.

Finally, it is my prayer that each person who uses these studies will come to know the joy and growth that comes from daily studying God's Word.

Suggestions for Leaders

The leader's primary goal is not to teach but to lead a discussion in which the participants feel free to share discoveries from their private study of the Bible. A wise leader can encourage learning by:

1.   Trusting the Holy Spirit to work through her.

2.   Providing a warm atmosphere in which all are encouraged to share.

3.   Keeping the discussion "on track." The discussion should not be based on what people think but on what God's Word says. The lesson questions are designed to enable this. The leader can always ask, "How did you answer the next question?"

4.   Covering all the assigned passages and questions. This encourages the participants to finish the study.

5.   Maintaining this rule: Only those who have finished the week's assignment may share in the discussion. What better way to encourage study?

6.   Shortening or rephrasing the questions, when necessary, for the sake of time or interest.

7.   Varying the method. Some questions will lend themselves to discussion. At other times, an answer from one person may be sufficient. Sometimes observations from several women may broaden the group's understanding.

8.   Summarizing the lesson. Some groups like the leader to summarize the lesson. A summary should give both the biblical principles found in the passages and the applications that specifically relate to the group's needs.

Introduction to Proverbs

"Many approach Proverbs as only a practical approach to living, that is, how to raise children, how to be successful, how to get along with neighbors . . . . But the main purpose is to give us the key to becoming people of wisdom." —Dr. Ronald Allen

The framework of the book of Proverbs under-scores this strategic purpose.

Framework of Proverbs

At first glance, Proverbs may appear to be arranged in a rather disorganized way so that the development of the book appears confusing. However, a type of order unveils when the first nine chapters are viewed as the introduction to the book. These chapters furnish the basis or perspective through which the rest of the book can be understood.

In the introductory section, an anonymous author reveals himself as a conscientious father (in the tradition of Deuteronomy 6:6–9), desirous of instructing his son concerning how to live life the very best way. Realizing that his son must first be motivated and prepared before he will listen to wisdom, the wise father-author sets the stage in chapters 1–9 to create a desire within his son (and, in turn, us) for the details of wisdom that will follow in the rest of the book.

Then in chapters 10–31 it may well be that the father turns editor, bringing together under the guidance of the Holy Spirit what had previously been several separate collections of wisdom sayings of the monarchs. Therefore, the separate collections of Solomon's proverbs in chapters 10:1–22:16, that of the wise men in 24:23–24, the collection of Solomon's sayings compiled by an editorial group of men commissioned by Hezekiah, chapters 23, 25–29, 31, the words of Agur 30:1–33, and the words of King Lemuel 31:1–9 are now brought together into one book.

The Spirit of God has seen to it that only truth is preserved in this united collection. What holds the entire book together is the author's aim to show how wise women and men can turn from death to life by submitting to God's ways (i.e., the fear of the Lord). This is wisdom!

Proverbs is Wisdom Literature

The book of Proverbs is part of the Wisdom Literature of the Old Testament that traditionally includes Job, Ecclesiastes, and Proverbs because these three have
*   a common vocabulary
*   a common world view: divine order established in the world by the creator
*   a common character: international and humanistic in contrast to the national Jewish and covenant character of the rest of the Old Testament.

All wisdom literature is in the form of poetry to strike a chord in the reader's or listener's heart and create a response. However, it is important to realize that the poetry of Proverbs is in parallelisms of "thought-rhyme" (lines arranged in pairs of *thought* rather than *sound*). For example: "The wise woman builds her house, but the foolish one tears it down with her own hands." Or "A gentle answer turns away wrath, but a harsh word stirs up anger."

What is a Proverb?

"A proverb is a brief but vivid statement of reality that causes the hearer to reflect upon a proper perspective of practical everyday human condition that might otherwise remain obscure and incomprehensible"

(Bruce Waltke). Biblical proverbs show us God's wisdom on how best to live everyday life.

Characteristics of Proverbs

• They don't argue, they assert (a declaration of fact).

• The tone of Proverbs is universal (general truth is presented).

• Their outlook is comprehensive (almost every human relationship is touched).

• They contain no unscientific statements (e.g., Proverbs 6:6–7).

• They are all on the highest moral plane, in contrast to other oriental proverbs.

• They are true to life (e.g., Proverbs 25:24).

The book of Proverbs is quoted over 60 times in the New Testament.

Who Wrote Proverbs?

It is only natural to be curious about the authors of Proverbs. The author of the introductory section remains anonymous, though he most likely was a high official or courtier.

The main body of Proverbs was written by Solomon, thus the title of the collection (see Proverbs 1:1) and the sections beginning with Proverbs 10:1 and Proverbs 25:1 bear his name.

Solomon was the son of King David by Bathsheba (2 Samuel 12:24, 1 Chronicles 3:5). After his father died, Solomon became the king of Israel ruling from 965 to 925 B.C. As the new king, Solomon humbly petitioned the Lord for wisdom and God specifically answered his request. The genius of God's gift to Solomon is reflected in the book of Proverbs.

Although Solomon is the main author of the book, a group of men referred to as "the wise men" wrote Proverbs 22:17 through 24:34. (See 1 Kings 4:31 for a reference to this class of men.)

Proverbs 25 through 29 were written by Solomon as well, but this section was put together 250 years later by an editorial group commissioned by King Hezekiah (700 B.C.), thus their name "men of Hezekiah." In chapter 30 we find the words of Agur and in 31:1–9 those of King Lemuel. Nothing more than their names is known of these two men.

Outline of Proverbs

Title, Introduction, and Motto (1:1–7)
I.   A father's praise of wisdom (1:8–9:18)
II.   Proverbs of Solomon (10:1–22:16)
III. a.   Words of the wise men (22:17–24:22)
      b.   Further words of wise men (24:23–24)
IV.   Further proverbs of Solomon (25:1–29:27)
      (Hezekiah's Collection)
V.   Words of Agur (30:1–33)
VI.   Words of King Lemuel (31:1–9)
VII. An alphabet of wifely excellence (31:10–31)

Lesson 1

Introduction to Biblical Wisdom

"Where can wisdom be found? Where does understanding dwell?" Job 28:12

When our world tries to answer this question various suggestions are made. Some say that wisdom is found in education, or certain people, or human experience. Others think it is discovered in old age or bought with silver and gold. The problem is not with these things in themselves; but wisdom cannot be defined by them.

The Scriptures state that wisdom begins with God and His perspective.

"God understands the way to it and He alone knows where it dwells." Job 28:23

So when a person earnestly confides, as my daughter did, "I want to be wise," to what do I direct her?

The book of Proverbs throws out the challenge: Do you want to be wise? Then here's the path.

"Wisdom calls: `You who are simple, gain prudence; you who are foolish, gain understanding. Listen, for I have worthy things to say; I open my lips to speak what is right. My mouth speaks what is true. . . . Choose my instruction instead of silver, knowledge rather than choice gold, for wisdom is more precious than rubies, and nothing you desire can compare with her' " (Proverbs 8:5, 6, 7, and 11).

Study Lesson 1

Daily Discovery I **In Search of Wisdom**

Stop and ask God to give you understanding as you study.

1. a. The route to becoming wise is often misunderstood. Genesis 3:1–6 records an interesting discussion between the serpent-Satan and Eve. In light of Genesis 3:1–6 (especially verse 6), what did Eve desire?

b. How did Eve attempt to get what she desired? In what way was this attempt inconsistent with the first principle of wisdom found in Proverbs 1:7? (Psalm 111:10 may help you.)

c. State the end result of Eve's approach to "getting" wisdom.

d. Can you think of a way you have been led astray on your search for wisdom?

2. Many years later, the suffering Job also desired to know wisdom. During interaction with friends, Job shared his conclusions concerning man's wisdom (Job 28:1–13). Through suffering, Job realized man is skillful in discovering treasures of earth, yet he does not easily know wisdom. Briefly summarize Job's perceptive conclusions in Job 28:13–28.

3. Two distinct types of wisdom are discussed in James 3:13–18. Describe each, indicating their end result. (Use a dictionary to broaden

your understanding of the descriptive words used in the passage. Share your research with the group.)

4. How could you use James 3:13–18 to help determine if a person is wise and understanding? In contrast, what guidelines are commonly are used?

Daily Discovery II **God, the Source of All Wisdom**

5. a. Summarize what the Scriptures declare concerning God in Daniel 2:20–22, Romans 16:27, and Colossians 2:2–3.

   b. On the basis of these verses, from whom should you first seek counsel in any situation? Do you?

   c. In what area do you need to apply this principle?

The discovery of wisdom must begin with God. If Eve had remembered the character of her God, she would not have been fooled into thinking that wisdom could be found apart from Him and His commands!

Daily Discovery III **Facets of Wisdom**

   "Wisdom is the principle thing," states Proverbs 4:1. It is helpful to understand wisdom's many facets as presented in Proverbs. The following words are used interchangeably with "wisdom" in Proverbs 1:1–5, helping the reader develop an understanding of the shades of meaning in this word, leading to a more complete picture of wisdom.

6. **Instruction** or **Training**. (Proverbs 1:2a, 3a) The use of this word is an indication that wisdom is not "picked-up" casually, like a pebble on the beach. The concept of time and discipline are suggested by the word **instruction**. This word usually has a note of sternness, ranging from warning to chastening.

Proverbs 24:30–32 is a good example of this concept concerning wisdom.

a. How was the author of Proverbs 24:30–32 warned by what he saw?

b. What wise response did the author have when he saw something that disturbed him?

c. How are you warned by this picture?

7. **Understanding** or **Insight**. Here the concept is one of discernment, since both nouns come from the verb "to discern."

a. When Solomon became king he asked the Lord for wisdom to lead the people. For what does 1 Kings 3:9 specify that Solomon asked?

b. In the New Testament, how is this same concept seen in Paul's prayer for believers in Philippians 1:9–10?

c. According to Hebrews 5:14, to become mature in Christ what area of your life needs training? What does the word "practice" in this verse suggest to you?

8. **Wise dealing** or **wise behavior**; common sense, practical wisdom.

a. In what way is the son of Proverbs 10:5 demonstrating this facet of wisdom?

b. How might you apply this proverb to your life?

9. **Discretion** and **Shrewdness** (not used in the negative sense here). The positive side of these words are used in Proverbs to show that a godly individual is one who takes the trouble to know her way about and plan her course realistically—"she knows the ropes."

How is this practical facet of wisdom seen in Proverbs 22:3? Try to make your answer personal.

10. **Knowledge** and **Learning**. Knowledge implies a knowing of truth, especially the truth concerning God. Learning emphasizes that truth is something given and then grasped.

In light of how **knowledge** is used in Proverbs (see above definition), what is Proverbs 2:6 declaring to those who say, "finite people can never be sure of anything concerning God?" What does this mean to you?

Daily Discovery IV **Expressions of Wisdom (Part 1)**

Proverbs may be expressed in a number of ways. Various types of proverbs may admonish, instruct, or observe lessons from life. The following will help you understand the variety of ways truth is expressed in the Proverbs.

11. A **comparative proverb** describes or defines one thing by comparing it to another. Most proverbs use comparison to teach their truths. The Hebrew word for **proverb** means "to be like" or "to represent" and is used for all expressions that compare one thing to another.

    a.   What is being compared in Proverbs 25:28?

    b.   Why might the picture presented in this proverb help you to grasp the proverb's meaning?

    c.   To what areas of your life might this proverb refer?

12. A **precept** is a rule concerning moral conduct and is often expressed as a command.

    a.   What is the wise or godly behavior commanded in Proverbs 25:21?

    b.   How might you apply this precept to your life? Be specific—insert a name.

13. A **maxim** is a rule emphasizing the practical aspects of life, often expressed as a command.

    a.   What practical truth is expressed in Proverbs 25:16–17?

    b.   Rewrite this maxim in your own words, relating it to a specific situation in your life.

14. A **truism** is a more or less universal truth that is applicable to many situations.

Restate the truism of Proverbs 10:4, making its meaning personal in your life.

15. An **adage** is a simple, practical truth expressed in a figure of speech.

a. Discover the truth expressed in the metaphor of Proverbs 25:4–5.

b. What wise counsel is God giving you through this proverb?

16. A **by-word** is a scornful or sarcastic exclamation about some object or person.

a. What is being emphasized in Proverbs 21:24? How?

b. Can you think of any situation in which this pictures you?

Daily Discovery V **Expressions of Wisdom (Part 2)**

17. An **admonition** does not leave it up to the reader to draw a conclusion, in contrast to a proverbial saying.

a. Explain the admonition in Proverbs 27:2. Can you think of an area of your life to which this admonition is particularly applicable?

b. Often the author adds a motive to his admonition as a basis for heeding the admonition. What is the clear admonition in

Proverbs 16:3? What motive is given to encourage this good work in you?

c. Consider an area of your life in which you are presently struggling (victory over a negative habit, reaching out to a problem person, a desire to properly encourage your husband), then follow the biblical admonition of Proverbs 16:3. Write out the verse, including your situation within it.

18. The **instructive saying** expresses a cause-effect relationship. The author presumes that his hearer will desire the "beneficial" effect rather than the "destructive."

a. In Proverbs 11:24 what is the cause and effect in each part of the comparison.

b. Which is the beneficial effect?

19. In the **sentence** or **saying** the author describes things "as they are," but the value of that which he is trying to impress upon the mind is not clear from the saying itself. In such cases the author's intention must be discovered from the overall emphasis of the book.

a. Read Proverbs 10:15, which is an example of a saying in which the author's intention might not be clear.

b. Is the author teaching that people should pursue wealth or security? Consider this interpretation in light of Proverbs 18:10–11 and 23:4–5 and then write out what you think the author of Proverbs 10:15 is teaching.

Notes For Study Lesson 1:

_____

_____

_____

_____

_____

_____

_____

_____

_____

_____

_____

_____

_____

_____

_____

_____

_____

_____

_____

_____

_____

_____

_____

_____

Woman of Wisdom

Lesson 2

Wisdom's Key and Requirements
(Proverbs 1 and 2)

The Fear of the Lord

God reveals the beginning place for wisdom through the theme call of Proverbs, "Fear the LORD!" After the initial challenge in Proverbs 1:7, the rest of the book unfolds the "how" of fearing the Lord in the details of life.

The concept of fear in Proverbs 1:7 is not one of terror or dread but one of reverence for God because of who He is. This type of reverence leads to a genuine desire to turn from evil and be obedient to God and His ways. In other words, true reverence for God produces a response of obedience or submission. It might help to look at the fear of the Lord this way:

Realizing who God is
leads
to
Reverential Awe = Fear of the Lord
leads
to
Response of Obedience or Submission
to the Majesty and Authority of God

The statement "the fear of the LORD is the beginning of knowledge" reveals the distinctive of the biblical proverbs in contrast to all other proverbs. It is the goal of Proverbs to give detailed instructions concerning what it is to "fear the LORD" in the daily events of life. This is how to live God's way.

Good and Evil

The wisdom revealed in Proverbs helps develop a God-given understanding of what is true about how life ought to be lived and what is false. Since wisdom involves living skillfully, a woman who would be wise must develop and respond to a sharpened awareness of what is good and what is evil. This is especially crucial in today's blurry world.

The introductory section of Proverbs—chapters 1 through 9—sets good against evil in strong contrast. Through a series of messages by the father-author, the issue of good and evil is set before the son. One of the father's teaching techniques is to personify good and evil as two women. The father contrasts "wisdom," the virtuous woman, with "sin," the strange woman or harlot who probably typifies all sin. In this section, as well as the whole book, "the good" is represented by several words: *wisdom, instruction, understanding, justice, judgment, equity, knowledge, discretion, learning, counsel.* The word *wisdom* is used most frequently— occurring 17 times in Proverbs 1–9 and 22 times in the rest of the book.

Chapters 1 through 9 discuss wisdom over and over again. As we read, we may be tempted to view wisdom as a vague, super-pious abstract. "Ah yes, I'll follow wisdom's way," and, "Oh yes, you follow it too . . . whatever it is!"

Let's be specific. Wisdom is God-given insight into good (how to live) and evil (how not to live). God's commands reveal the way to live the good life (Deuteronomy 5:29); therefore, following wisdom equals doing God's commands. Let's say, for example, that someone has wronged you. Wisdom calls, "Do not let the sun go down while you are still angry." Immediately you are faced with a decision—wisdom's way or your own. Or let's say that the present circumstances of your life are dismal, discouraging, depressing. Your mind wants to focus on how bad things are, and wisdom gently reminds you, "You will keep in perfect peace him whose mind is steadfast." We have a choice. Wisdom encourages us, "Eat at my table." "Make your ear attentive to wisdom, incline your heart." How practical this is to a student of the Scripture. Everyday, in a thousand ways, the call of wisdom is heard: follow God's ways, for they are good!

Study Lesson 2

Daily Discovery I **The Value of Proverbs (Proverbs 1:1–6)**

(As you begin to study Proverbs, I suggest that you start a practical subject notebook listing verse references under such relevant topic headings as "Gossip," "Children," and "Money." Use the pages in the back of this book to get started.)

1.   The reasons why the book of Proverbs was written are given in Proverbs 1:2–3. List these inserting your own name before each reason (e.g., that Mary may attain wisdom . . .).

2.   a.   Read Proverbs 1:4–6. Using these verses, indicate the types of people to whom Proverbs will be of great value. Alongside each type, state what the study of Proverbs will do for them.

     b.   With which type do you most closely relate? What then does the Scripture promise will be the value of the study of Proverbs to you?

Daily Discovery II **The Theme of Proverbs (Proverbs 1:7)**

3.   What key statement is given in Proverbs 1:7 that discloses the beginning point of your becoming a truly wise woman? (It is this theme that sets the biblical proverbs apart from all other proverbs.)

4. Put in your own words the meaning of the phrase "the fear of the LORD," after consulting Proverbs 2:5, 9:10, 14:27, 23:17, as well as Job 28:28 and Psalm 111:10.

5.   By comparing Proverbs 1:7 with Psalm 37:30, what specific things can you learn about a woman who "opens her mouth in wisdom."

6.   What could you say about the cliche, "She was born wise." Is wisdom inherited or acquired? Base your answer on the truths found in Proverbs 1:7, 2:6, Psalm 51:6b, and James 1:5.

Daily Discovery III **Warning Concerning Sin's Enticement (Proverbs 1:8–19)**

7.   Immediately after the statement of Proverbs 1:7 comes a warning to the disciple of wisdom (Proverbs 1:8–19). Briefly describe the behavior of alluring individuals who entice others down a path of sin.

8.   a.   What is the end result of following their "path?" (Proverbs 1:18–19).

b.   Can you think of any individuals who are an example of this end?

9.   a.   What clear instruction does the father give concerning the response to enticement? (Proverbs 1:10, 15).

b.   In what ways are you enticed to sin? Relate the instructions of Proverbs 1:10 and 15 to your situation and be specific about what you can do.

10. List wisdom's rewards to you when you do not give in to enticement (Proverbs 3:1–26, 33–35). As you write, put your own name into each reward.

Daily Discovery IV **Personification of Wisdom (Proverbs 1:20–33)**

a.   Read through the picture Proverbs 1:20–33 gives of God's wisdom.

b.   From this personification of wisdom, would you say that God is trying to hide or be secretive about His wisdom? Explain, giving verses to support your answer.

12. In light of this description, what do you think will be the majority's response to wisdom's cry? Note particularly the verbs of response.

13. According to the passage, is it wisdom's fault if the fool and the scorner end up in trouble? Explain your answer. (Verses 30 and 31 may help you.)

Daily Discovery V **Prerequisites for a Woman of Wisdom (Proverbs 2:1–19)**

"Wisdom is the principal thing," states Proverbs 4:7. In his commentary on Proverbs Derek Kidner's apt paraphrase of this verse reads, "What it takes is not brains or opportunity but decision. Do you want it? Come and get it."

14. a.   Proverbs 2:1–4 sets forth what you need to do to become a woman of wisdom. Name the important "ifs" or conditions given in these verses.

     b.   Since these conditions are so crucial to your study of this book, write out a brief definition for each. (A dictionary may help you.) As you do, relate the particular action involved to yourself.

15. Proverbs 2:5–9 reveals that you will become discerning in what areas if you personally give heed to God's prerequisites for wisdom? ("To discern" in Proverbs 2:5, 9 means to gain insight, to observe with perception.)

16. When Proverbs 2:1–9 begins to take place in your heart, what is God's faithful yet amazing promise to you in Proverbs 2:10–11? Make your answer personal by using the word **my** in your answer.

17. What two major deliverances come from this godly discernment? (Proverbs 2:11–19, especially 2:12 and 16). In what specific area(s) of your life do you need this type of deliverance now?

Woman of Wisdom

Notes For Study Lesson 2:

_____
_____
_____
_____
_____
_____
_____
_____
_____
_____
_____
_____
_____
_____
_____
_____
_____
_____
_____
_____
_____
_____
_____
_____
_____
_____

Lesson 2: *Wisdom's Key and Requirements*

Woman of Wisdom

Lesson 3

Like Father, Like Son
(Proverbs 3 and 4)

"These commandments that I give you today are to be upon your hearts. Impress them on your children. Talk about them when you sit at home and when you walk along the road, when you lie down and when you get up" (Deuteronomy 6:6–7).

It appears from the passage for this week's study (Proverbs 3 and 4) that the Lord's words in Deuteronomy are heeded in the household of the editor-author of Proverbs. He was taught the commands of God by his father (Proverbs 4:3–5) and now he is teaching his son how to live right, "That it might be well with [him] and [his] children forever" (Deuteronomy 5:29). "The linking of these three generations demonstrates how the love of the best things will be transmitted mainly by personal influence, along the channels of affection" (*Proverbs*, Kidner). The truth of this statement came home to me when I read my great grandfather's journal. I was struck by his reverence for God and his decisions to follow God's ways through difficulty and delight. I ponder the fact that his descendants also desired to know God.

Along with teaching the ways of wisdom, both fathers show they understand that commands and admonitions about how to live are meaningless to one whose heart attitude is not right before God. Therefore, the section also emphasizes an attitude of humble response (submission) and teachableness (the awareness that you are not always right), that wisdom might be heard and her ways followed.

In the Old Testament Jewish family, all instruction took place in the home under the father's leadership. However, Proverbs reveals an important feature of that home education. The biblical proverbs refer to mothers as companion instructors.

"Listen, my son, to your father's instruction and do not forsake your mother's teaching" (Proverbs 1:8).

"My son, observe your father's commands and do not forsake your mother's teaching" (Proverbs 6:20).

The book of Proverbs is unique among all wisdom literature of the ancient Near East because of its references to the mother as a teacher of her child. Proverbs sets forth a household in which both the father and the mother share as one in the instruction of their children. And so it is to be today!

Study Lesson 3

Daily Discovery I **A Parent's Obedience (Proverbs 3)**

1. Deuteronomy 6:6–8 gives parents clear direction regarding their unceasing responsibility for instructing their children.

 a. In what ways were the fathers of Proverbs 3:1–4 and Proverbs 4:1–4 obedient to the commands of Deuteronomy 6:6–8?

 b. In these verses, what is the obvious result of their obedience to the Deuteronomy 6:6–9 command?

 c. Can you think of one specific way you might implement the instructions of Deuteronomy 6:6–7 with your child or with a child?

2.   a.   What do you think is meant by the phrase in Proverbs 3:4, "favor and a good name in the sight of God and man?" (Proverbs 3:3 and 4, 32, 8:32, 1 Samuel 2:26, Luke 2:51–52, and Psalm 111:10 may help you.)

   b.   In light of the verses above, what should parents be doing to stress with their children the value of a good name?

Daily Discovery II   **The Outworking (Proverbs 3:1–12)**

3.   Proverbs 3:1–12 is a very encouraging and instructive passage. Every odd numbered verse gives a command for us to heed and to teach our children. Every even numbered verse provides a motive for heeding that command. Using the following columns, summarize each command and its accompanying encouragement. As you do this, star the verses that seem especially meaningful to you to share with your child or a friend.

The Command	**The Motive**
3:1	3:2
3:3	3:4
3:5	3:6
3:7	3:8
3:9	3:10

Daily Discovery III   **Wisdom's Effect (Proverbs 3:13–26)**

4.   Read Proverbs 3:13–26 and list the various effects that wisdom will have upon your life.

Lesson 3: Like Father, Like Son

Daily Discovery IV **Knowing God in Action**
(Proverbs 3:27–35)

5.   Chapter 3 concludes with specific examples
of what it means to know God "in all your ways"
(See Proverbs 3:6). In your own words
summarize each example, making application to
your own life where possible (Proverbs 3:27–35).

Daily Discovery V **The Two Paths**
(Proverbs 4)

6.   In Proverbs 4, the father's intention is to
motivate his son to discover what he himself
discovered—that real living is tied to growing in
wisdom. (As you read, note the emotions that
accompany the father's counsel.) To encourage
his son to make this discovery, what does the
father tell his son to do? (Proverbs 4:5–9). Are
you in the process of doing these things? How?

7.   In Proverbs 4:10–19 the wisdom writer
presents two paths. He helps us see that we
must decide between them.
     a.   What might the path of Proverbs
4:10–13 be called?
     b.   Name the path of Proverbs 4:14–17.
     c.   Using your own words, tell how the two
paths are compared in Proverbs 4:18 and 19?

8.   If you were to respond to the key command
of the introductory section of Proverbs (1:8),
what would you be doing according to Proverbs
4:20–27? Are you willing to ask God to enable
you to do this? If so, ask now.

Notes For Study Lesson 3:

_____

_____

_____

_____

_____

_____

_____

_____

_____

_____

_____

_____

_____

_____

_____

_____

_____

_____

_____

_____

_____

_____

_____

_____

_____

Lesson 3: Like Father, Like Son

Woman of Wisdom

Lesson 4

Worldly Wise
(Proverbs 5, 6, and 7)

The frank discussion of sin in Proverbs 5, 6, and 7 is graphic. And it is as immensely practical to us today as it was in Old Testament times. In these chapters, it is as if the glamorous coverlet of sin is pulled back, revealing the decay beneath. Truths about sin are revealed symbolically through the figure of the seductive woman of sin who lures her victims with honey-coated words of death. Looking at this woman, the author analyzes the attraction and artificial lure of sin that offer quick but unsatisfying pleasures (Proverbs 5). His observations lead to specific warnings and counsel against the tragic waste of sin's traps (Proverbs 6), as well as to the practical emphasis of how to prepare for temptation (Proverbs 7).

Though the seductress represents sexual immorality in particular, application may be made to other forms of temptation.

"Open my eyes that I may see wonderful things in your law" (Psalm 119:18).

Study Lesson 4

Daily Discovery I **The Trick of Sin (Proverbs 5)**

Before introducing the discussion of sin in Proverbs 5 through 7, the author gives an important command. If heeded, this command would protect against sin. Wisely, the author gives motivation for obedience to the command by indicating the specific good result that will follow. He also gives clear explanation for the command's need.

1.   Discover this practical command, the reason for it, and the result of obedience in Proverbs 5:1–3.

2.   Describe in your own words what lies under the exterior attractiveness of the "adulteress." Can you think of other temptations (perhaps some to which you are especially attracted) that might be described similarly?

3.   a.   List the results of succumbing to the "adulteress" (Proverbs 5:7–14).

     b.   According to these verses how can you protect yourself?

4.   As you read Proverbs 5:15–23, note the vivid contrast to the pathetic picture of Proverbs 5:7–14. What do you think is the main message of verses 15–23? What words in this passage seem to show the greatest contrast with the misery of Proverbs 5:7–14?

Daily Discovery II   **Wisdom's Counsel Against Sin (Proverbs 6)**

5.   Read Proverbs 6:1–5, 6–11, 12–15, 23–35. Discover the main subject of each paragraph. Are any of these areas "traps" for you?

6. a. Proverbs 6:16–19 details seven abominations to God. How would you define the word **abomination**? (A dictionary may help you.)

   b. With one word summarize each abomination.

7. According to Proverbs 6:20–23, what will protect you from temptation or help you in the midst of it? How might you do this? Be specific.

Daily Discovery III **Preparation for Temptation (Proverbs 7:1–5)**

8. a. In Proverbs 7 the father shares with his son a tragic drama of succumbing to temptation. First, however, the father reveals to his son specific things that can be a living and powerful force to keep him from an end similar to the young man in the illustration. What are these? (Note that the father did the same thing in Proverbs 5:1–3.)

   b. In light of 1 Corinthians 10:12, why are the principles found in Proverbs 7:1–3 and 24–26 also important for us to remember? Consider a specific way in which you might apply each principle to your life.

9. Again and again God's Word gives us examples of what can occur when His principles are ignored. Explain what happened to the famous man of wisdom, King Solomon, when he no longer applied the truths of Proverbs 7:1–3. (1 Kings 3:5–15, 11:1–4)

Daily Discovery IV **The Seduction by the Woman of Sin (Proverbs 7:6–23)**

10. After reading Proverbs 7:6–9, how would you describe the character of the victim in the illustration? Do you know anyone like this?

11. In your own words, describe the type of person the young man meets in the darkness. (Get your information from Proverbs 7:10–12.)

12. a. By what methods does the seductress lure her victim? See Proverbs 7:13–21.

b. Explain the effect these methods have upon the young man. Proverbs 7:22–23.

13. In light of Proverbs 5:1–3, what is wrong with the young man of Proverbs 7:6–12?

Daily Discovery V **The Cost of Sin (Proverbs 7:24–27)**

14. What will it cost the young man if he follows the woman of sin? Use these verses to help you answer: Proverbs 2:18, 5:5, 6:32, 7:26–27, 9:18.

15. Name some specific principles you have learned from Proverbs 7 that help you counsel your children, friends, or yourself.

Notes For Study Lesson 4:

_____

_____

_____

_____

_____

_____

_____

_____

_____

_____

_____

_____

_____

_____

_____

_____

_____

_____

_____

_____

_____

_____

_____

_____

_____

_____

_____

Lesson 4: _Worldly Wise_

Woman of Wisdom

Lesson 5

Wisdom Serves Food for Thought—Part 1 (Proverbs 8)

What a contrast! Luringly the woman of sin in chapters 5, 6, and 7 invites the naive into the blackness of her house, promising that "stolen water is sweet; food eaten in secret is delicious." She deceives the unwary with honey-coated words that hide the death they bring.

In vivid contrast is the brilliant call in Proverbs 8 and 9 of the woman of wisdom, "Come eat of my food!" Wisdom invites us to a healthy, life-giving banquet table.

Wisdom is the key word of the book. It has been the author's purpose to imprint the meaning and path of wisdom upon our minds. Thus the author has repeatedly shown that life apart from following God's ways is no life at all. Wisdom begins the moment we start to reverence God ("the fear of the LORD"), submitting to God by following His commands. The doing of God's Word is the path of wisdom that "shines brighter and brighter until the full day." The way of the wicked gets progressively darker until it ends in destruction. We have no other choices. Proverbs 1 through 9 has stripped all the gray alternatives away and said, "This is it; it's either one way or the other! Which way will *you* go?" The authors intend to stir a decision within us.

The author is not casual about his son's choice (and ours). He wants us to realize that the decision is one of everlasting consequence. Wisdom calls out: "He who finds me, finds life. Those who hate me love death."

In case we have missed the point, the author draws his introduction to the book to a dramatic conclusion. He throws the spotlight on folly's secret house, that the dead inside might be revealed.

Study Lesson 5

Daily Discovery I **The Great Contrast (Proverbs 7 and 8)**

1. Read Proverbs 7 and 8.

2. To see wisdom clearly "the woman" of Proverbs 8 and 9 is set in strong contrast to the woman of Proverbs 5–7.

   a. Compare their names: Proverbs 6:26 and 7:5 **and** Proverbs 8:1, 12.

   b. Compare from where they call: Proverbs 7:12 **and** Proverbs 8:2–3 and 1:20–21.

   c. Compare their messages: Proverbs 7:5 **and** Proverbs 8:6–8.

   d. Compare their promises: Proverbs 7:16–18 **and** Proverbs 8:21, 35 and 9:11. In particular, what do the comparisons mentioned in c. and d. mean to you personally?

   e. Compare the results of your heeding: Proverbs 7:26–27 **and** Proverbs 8:35 and 9:6, 11.

   f. Briefly summarize the major contrast between the two women.

Daily Discovery II **Wisdom's Gifts**
(Proverbs 8)

3. a. What types of people does wisdom offer to change? See Proverbs 8:5.

b. In light of today's world, why are wisdom's words strategic? See Proverbs 8:6–9.

4. a. What two benefits does wisdom offer you in Proverbs 8:10? (Read this verse aloud, inserting your own name, i.e., "Mary choose my . . . and . . .")

b. How might we today choose "silver and gold" over wisdom's gifts? Give examples.

c. What is the paradox of such a choice? See Proverbs 8:11, 18–21.

5. a. To get understanding we must "fear the LORD" (Proverbs 1:7). In what way does our study's definition of the fear of the Lord (submission to the majesty and authority of God that results in following His ways) relate to the statement of Proverbs 8:13?

b. If you hate evil, from what four things will you turn? See Proverbs 8:13.

c. Why do you think that it might be particularly important that a child understand these things? See Proverbs 22:6.

6. a. What other possessions does wisdom have that she will share with those who love her? See Proverbs 8:14–16.

b.   Who is shown to possess these same characteristics? Job 12:13, Isaiah 11:1–2.

c.   As you reflect on the Proverbs, Job, and Isaiah passages above, to what conclusion do you come? Make a personal response here.

Daily Discovery III **Wisdom's Presence in Creation (Proverbs 8:22–31)**

This section is "not designed to preoccupy the reader with metaphysics, but to stir him to a decision" (Kidner).

7. a.   Read carefully Proverbs 8:22–31. Summarize wisdom's role in creation.

b.   Whose wisdom is being personified in Proverbs 8:22–31? Support your answer by referring to John 1:1–14, 1 Corinthians 1:24–30, Colossians 1:15–17, 2:3, Hebrews 1:1–4, and Revelation 3:14.

Daily Discovery IV **The Decision (Proverbs 8:32–36)**

At the conclusion of chapter 8 we are brought to a "now then . . ." in verse 32 which is directed to each of us. We are meant to be stirred to a decision.

8. a.   No matter what type of person you are (see Proverbs 8:5), according to Proverbs 8:32–36 what decision are you to make? Have you made this decision?

b. If you sincerely want to be wise, what are you to do according to Proverbs 8:17, 34? Explain each activity in terms of your own life. (For example, looking up the word "diligent" in a dictionary might help you, as well as considering what it might mean to watch daily at wisdom's gates.)

9. What positive assurance is given to the sincere seeker who has made the above decision? See Proverbs 8:17, 34–35 and James 1:5–8.

Daily Discovery V **The One Necessity in Life (Proverbs 8:32–36)**

10. a. In light of Proverbs 8:32–36, what is the one necessity of life?

b. How do you think you could convey this truth to those around you (i.e., at home, school, work, neighborhood)?

11. Explain how Jesus' words in John 14:6, and the statements of John 1:12 and 1 John 5:11–13, relate to the discoveries you have made in Proverbs 8.

Notes For Study Lesson 5:

_____

_____

_____

_____

Lesson 6

Wisdom Serves Food for Thought—Part 2 (Proverbs 9)

It is special to be invited to a banquet, but Proverbs 9 cautions us to be careful at which one we are seated! In this chapter both Wisdom and Folly invite guests to respective tables. Wisdom's banquet provides healthy, life-producing food. Folly's banquet promises "sweet" and "delicious" food, but eating at her table will kill you! This chapter is very practical today, for both invitations go out daily.

Study Lesson 6

Daily Discovery I **The Two Banquets (Proverbs 9:1–9)**

1. As a single woman, or wife, or mother, why would you personally want to attend wisdom's banquet? Give at least two specific reasons based on Proverbs 9.

2. a. According to Proverbs 9:6, how does one get to wisdom's banquet?

   b. How can you "proceed in the way of understanding?" (In other words, stay at the banquet.) Proverbs 8:32–36 will help you. Make one application of these instructions to your life.

Woman of Wisdom

Daily Discovery II **The Two Mottos (Proverbs 9:10–18)**

3.   Proverbs 9:10 has been called the theme song of the wise. Restate that motto here, inserting your own name.

After considering Proverbs 9:13–18, along with Proverbs 20:17, what "motto" might you give for folly's banquet? If possible, share your discovery with a child or teenager.

4.   List the similarities and the differences between the two feasts set forth in Proverbs 9. Why might it be important to be aware of both the similarities and differences of the two feasts?

5.   a.   In the middle of the discussion of the two banquets, Proverbs 9:7–12 reveals the characteristics that result from attending each. What are they? Apply the challenge of these verses to your life.

b.   In your own words, explain Proverbs 9:8–9.

6.   What shattering end results of attending folly's banquet dramatically conclude the introductory section of the Proverbs? See Proverbs 9:13–18, especially verse 18.

Daily Discovery III **Proverbs 9 Illustrated**

7.   After reflecting on Proverbs 9, consider one possible way to convey the important truths of this chapter to a friend, to a child. Carry out

your plan and then share the results with your group.

Daily Discovery IV and V **Application Action (Proverbs 1–9)**

8. As you have studied the introductory section of Proverbs (chapters 1–9), what key principles have been impressed on your mind? Take any two principles and develop a plan of action to apply them.

9. What decisions (or determinations) have resulted in your life from your progress so far in Proverbs? Take time to carefully list them here.

Notes For Study Lesson 6:

_____

_____

_____

_____

_____

_____

_____

_____

_____

_____

_____

_____

Woman of Wisdom

Lesson 7

Living Life Skillfully
(Proverbs 10 and 11)

Here we are! Wisdom is the pathway to life, and we made the decision to walk this path. Proverbs 4:18 explains that the road we're now on "is like the first gleam of dawn, shining ever brighter till the full light of day." What encouragement! Proverbs 1–9 provided the basis for our choice. In these chapters we discovered the core essential of the wise woman. She fears the Lord and commits her life to the path of wisdom, a path, she realizes, that can only be followed as she "trusts in the LORD with all [her] heart and leans not on [her] own understanding. In all [her] ways [she] acknowledges (knows) him" (Proverbs 3:5–6).

From this point on in our study, we will learn how the wise woman is to live. The emphasis of chapters 10–31 concerns how to "fear the LORD" in daily circumstances; in other words, godly living in the mundane. We are about to learn how to live life with skill. Though this portion reveals the best way to live, it is primarily written to show believers how they may please the Lord in even the small details of life.

Proverbs teaches through contrasts. In the first section the contrasts were expressed in long passages. Now, in the second section, the contrast is expressed in short, one-verse units, many of which have a "but" in the middle of the verse (e.g., "When pride comes, then comes disgrace, but with the humility comes wisdom" [Proverbs 11:2]) .

Woman of Wisdom

Study Lesson 7

Daily Discovery I **Ways to Fear the Lord (Proverbs 10)**

1. To see the strong contrast between wise living (godly living) and foolish existence (ungodly living), fill in the appropriate statements for each verse of Proverbs 10.

How to Fear the Lord (Live Wisely)	Foolish Living (Ungodly)
For Example: vs. 1 A wise son makes a father glad	A foolish son is a grief to his mother
vs. 2 Righteousness delivers from death	Ill-gotten gain does not profit

Daily Discovery II **The Mouth (Proverbs 10)**

2. As we begin to study the outworking of the fear of the Lord in everyday life, the mouth is emphasized. Discover what Proverbs 10 says about the mouth. Summarize your findings.

3. Using the journal pages in the back, add the heading "The Mouth" to your subject notebook. List what Proverbs 10 says about the mouth. You will want to add more under this heading as you continue through Proverbs.

4. a. How is the mouth of a righteous person described in Proverbs 10:11?

b. Explain more fully what this description means using Psalm 36:8–9 and Proverbs 13:14, 14:27, 16:22.

5. What do you think is meant by "the lips of the righteous feed many"? Proverbs 10:21.

6. Instead of "ill-gotten treasures" that do not profit (Proverbs 10:2), what can you find in Proverbs 10 that do profit?

7. Security is the key ingredient of peace. Proverbs 10:2–3, 27–30 mention different types of security that are yours when you walk in the way of righteousness. What are they?

Daily Discovery III **The Ways of the Upright and the ways of the Wicked (Proverbs 11)**

8. a. To show how important the subject of Proverbs 11:1 is, the law (Leviticus 19:35), the prophets (Micah 6:10), and the wisdom writings (Proverbs 16:11, 20:10, 23) all address it. Identify the subject and specific ways to apply it in your life.

b. Instead of the tendency reflected in Proverbs 11:1a, what is a Christian woman's attitude to be according to Luke 6:35–38?

Daily Discovery IV **Pride (Proverbs 11)**

9. Proverbs 11:2 reveals something very interesting. In this verse the word for **pride** is used of those who must have everything their own way. The word for **humble** refers to just the opposite. In light of this, what do you think the

proverb is saying about a woman of wisdom?
(See Micah 6:8 for the only other place this
word is used.)

10. God reveals many things about pride in the
book of Proverbs. Make an observation after
each of the following verses. Add "Pride" as a
heading in your subject notebook.
   a.   Proverbs 8:13
   b.   Proverbs 11:2
   c.   Proverbs 13:10
   d.   Proverbs 16:18
   e.   Proverbs 21:24
   f.   Proverbs 29:23

11. In what ways does living righteously assist
a person according to Proverbs 11:3–9?

Daily Discovery V **Delighting the Lord
(Proverbs 11:9–23)**

12. Proverbs 11:20 states, "The LORD detests
men of perverse heart but he delights in those
whose ways are blameless." Read Proverbs
11:9–23, noticing the actions that bring delight
to the Lord. Choose one specific way to walk
blamelessly. Consider that each time you do this
you delight God!

In Proverbs 11:9–23 two qualities of a
woman are singled out; one is positive, the other
negative. Using a dictionary, explain these
qualities.

13. Summarize practically the teaching
concerning generosity found in Proverbs
11:24–26.

Notes For Study Lesson 7:

_____

_____

_____

_____

_____

_____

_____

_____

_____

_____

_____

_____

_____

_____

_____

_____

_____

_____

_____

_____

_____

_____

Lesson 7: Living Life Skillfully

Woman of Wisdom

Lesson 8

Think it Over
(Proverbs 12 and 13)

"Misfortune pursues the sinner, but prosperity is the reward of the righteous" (Proverbs 13:21).

By now in your study of Proverbs you may have begun scratching your head and thinking, "Wait a minute. Proverbs says the righteous will prosper. I've seen the upright suffer! I've had friends not get a promotion or even lose their jobs on account of a godly stand. I've seen the businesses of the honest robbed."

It is important to realize the perspective from which the truth of Proverbs is to be viewed. The book shows that you cannot get to truth by observation and experience alone. Life cannot be judged in accordance with the moment; you and I must keep the end in view. The book of Proverbs reveals that "end" or ultimate outcome of righteousness. However, often we do not have to wait that long. "What was lost with paradise and waits to be regained can be enjoyed in some measure here and now when man walks with God" (Kidner). As we walk in righteousness, we experience eternal life now!

Study Lesson 8

Daily Discovery I **The Contrast**
(Proverbs 12)

1. Read Proverbs 12 and make a list of what the righteous do along with a list of what the

foolish do. Pick several truths and explain why they are meaningful to you.

The Righteous	The Fool
For example:	
vs. 1 Loves discipline	Hates reproof

2.   As you read through your "Fool" column, what determinations do you personally need to make to avoid becoming a fool?

Daily Discovery II   **Proverbs' Sketch of the Sluggard Selected (Proverbs 12)**

3.   Describe the character of the sluggard (i.e., his conduct, his excuses) from the following: Proverbs 6:9–11, 10:5, 26, 12:27, 13:4, 15:19, 18:9, 19:24, 20:4, 21:25–26, 22:13, 26:13–16.

    a.   What practical help does Proverbs offer a sluggard? See Proverbs 6:6 and 13:4.

    b.   What do you need to learn from the ant? Make application to a specific area of your life.

4.   As she studies Proverbs' portrayal of the sluggard, what does a wise woman do according to Proverbs 24:32? In what area of your life have you been challenged by the picture of the sluggard? What will you do about it? Explain one plan of action.

Daily Discovery III **The End Result**
(Proverbs 12)

5.   Paraphrase Proverbs 12:4 in terms relevant
to you.

6.   State a practical outworking of Proverbs
12:13 in your life.

7.   Look over Proverbs 12 and choose two of
the proverbs that are particularly instructive to
you. What will you do now?

Daily Discovery IV **Wisdom in Our Lives**
(Proverbs 13)

8.   To know the things a woman on wisdom's
righteous path does, read through Proverbs 13
and list each action. These are not to be left as
words on a page. They are written that they
might be translated into our lives. In a column
alongside, add any results of these wise actions
given in Proverbs 13. (Note how God motivates
us to choose wisely. Do you do the same?)

9.   Proverbs 13:4, "The sluggard craves and
gets nothing, but the desires of the diligent are
fully satisfied," and the rest of this chapter
emphasizes the use of earthly possessions in a
wise way. However, the chapter also makes clear
what the greatest earthly possession is. Discover
it in Proverbs 13:13–14. Why is this gift of God
to us such a precious possession according to
these verses? (See also Matthew 6:33 and
1 Peter 1:23–25.)

Daily Discovery V **A Woman and Her Words (Selected Proverbs)**

10. What do you think Proverbs 13:2-3 is saying about the words of a godly woman?

11. a.   Of the seven abominations to the Lord, how many have to do with words? Name them (Proverbs 6:16-19).

b.   Give an example of a seemingly harmless way each of these word abominations might show up in your daily life.

12. a.   One of the most powerful forces is the spoken word. What power do the following proverbs attribute to words: Proverbs 12:18, 25, 16:27-28, 18:8, 21?

b.   What new insights have you gained from these verses?

13. The statement "Evil words die without a welcome" relates to Proverbs 17:4. How? What personal challenge does this proverb have for you?

14. Though words are powerful, for what things are they not a substitute in light of Proverbs 14:23 and 29:19?

15. In your own words, describe the great contrast between Proverbs 10:21a and 11:9a.

16. Good words that are the result of choosing wisdom's route daily are characterized by: (Note margin in some translations.)

a. Proverbs 11:12–13 and 13:3
b. Proverbs 15:1 and 25:15
c. Proverbs 15:23
d. Proverbs 24:26

Notes For Study Lesson 8:

_____

_____

_____

_____

_____

_____

_____

_____

_____

_____

_____

_____

_____

_____

_____

_____

_____

_____

_____

_____

Lesson 8: Think it Over

Woman of Wisdom

Lesson 9

The Wise Character and The Foolish Character (Proverbs 14 and 15)

Proverbs 14 explores the basis for the wise and the foolish nature, as well as the result of each character. It is revealing to discover that certain behaviors accompany each nature: the wise woman builds her house, but with her own hands the foolish one tears hers down. We are cautioned here to consider seriously those attitudes and actions that lead to wisdom or folly. Our daily choices determine the kind of character being developed in us.

Study Lesson 9

Daily Discovery I **The Wise and the Foolish Character (Proverbs 14)**

1. As you read Proverbs 14, look for the two natures (the wise and the foolish). Record some of the end products of each character, noting those you particularly desire. Give verse reference.

Daily Discovery II **The Woman Who Builds Her House (Proverbs 14)**

2. One of the most important characteristics of the woman of wisdom is found in Proverbs 14:1. Since the major thrust of this proverb is not to

be understood in terms of a physical building, what do you think is its message?

3.   a.   Think of specific ways you as a woman of wisdom can "build your house" now.

     b.   Are there any ways you might be "tearing down your house" with your own hands?

4.   Though Proverbs emphasizes a diligence that would result in orderliness, it is not sterile orderliness. The healthy balance of God's ways is demonstrated by Proverbs 14:4, "Where there are no oxen, the manger is empty, but from the strength of an ox comes an abundant harvest." Put the theme of this proverb in words relevant to your life as a woman or homemaker.

5.   When you are tempted to believe that a lie is needed, what is the clear statement of Proverbs 14:25? Can you think of an illustration of this proverb?

6.   Contrast the serious warning in Proverbs 14:12 with the confidence found in Proverbs 14:26.

Daily Discovery III   **A Healthy Body (Selected Proverbs)**

7.   Make a new heading in your subject notebook, "A Healthy Body." Proverbs reveals what is healthy for your body and what is not. Start with Proverbs 14:30. Try rewriting this proverb in your own words after reading Proverbs 16:32, Proverbs 19:11, Ecclesiastes

7:9 and James 1:19. Begin noting "Healthy Body" proverbs as you continue through the book.

Daily Discovery IV **and V** **The Heart Attitude (Proverbs 15)**

8.   A woman's words, the tongue that speaks them, and the heart that chooses them, reveal much about her. Many of the proverbs of chapter 15 concern these three aspects of our characters. As you read through the chapter choose one proverb in each of these areas that seems especially relevant to you and derive an application to share with a member of your family or a friend. Share the three applications here. What responses did you encounter?

9.   Proverbs 15:13 shows that our prevailing attitude colors our whole personality, but verse 15 indicates that it also colors our whole experience. Explain this truth in terms of your life.

10. The heart attitude is also of crucial importance to God when it comes to worship and service that is acceptable to Him. (See Proverbs 15:8, 29.) Give specific reasons why "the LORD detests the sacrifice of the wicked." See Isaiah 29:13 and 1 Samuel 15:22.

11. Godly humility that comes before honor (Proverbs 15:33) is characterized in this chapter by the ability to accept life-giving reproof. Find the five verses that emphasize the necessity to submit yourself to reproof or correction for your faults.

Notes For Study Lesson 9:

Lesson 10

Never Alone
(Proverbs 16)

I don't know about you, but when I begin to look over Proverbs' "lists" of wise things and foolish, it gets a bit overwhelming.

"How can anyone do this?" I exclaim.

In asking that question, I have forgotten a major theme of the introductory section of Proverbs (chapters 1–9). The statements concerning how to live wisely were to be viewed and understood through the key perspective found in Proverbs 3:5–6:

> "Trust in the LORD with all your heart and lean not on your own understanding; in all your ways acknowledge him, and he will make your paths straight."

Dependence on God is the essential ingredient for the outworking of Proverbs in our lives. It is with this perspective before us that we must continue along wisdom's path. The "How to Live Wisely in Daily Life" theme continues from Proverbs 10 to the end of the book; yet, there is a change of style beginning in Proverbs 16.

In chapters 10–15 godly living was emphasized by contrast using the key word *but*. Now in chapters 16 through 22:16 godly living is stressed by repetition and addition. For example: "Commit to the LORD whatever you do, and your plans will succeed" (emphasis by addition) Proverbs 16:3. "Kings take pleasure in honest lips; they value a man who speaks the truth" (emphasis by repetition) Proverbs 16:13.

Study Lesson 10

Daily Discovery I **The Sovereignty of God (Proverbs 16)**

1.   One of the consistent truths of Scripture is that God is in control of all things; He is sovereign.

Record the specific truths you find in Proverbs 16:1–9, 33 that underscore God's role as sovereign King of all creation. (Be sure to state the supporting verse.) Explain how each demonstrates God's control over His creation.

2.   What do these truths suggest to you in terms of your own life? Choose one and relate it to your present situation.

Daily Discovery II **Blessed Responsibilities (Proverbs 16:1–16)**

3.   Rewrite Proverbs 16:6 in your own words.

4.   a.   Give the main theme of Proverbs 16:1, 9, 19:21, and 20:24.

b.   Explain the reason Jeremiah 10:23 gives as to why the Lord is needed. Make it personal by including your name in the answer.

c.   Why might someone be uncomfortable with the above truth?

d.   In what way is Proverbs 16:9 an encouragement to you?

5. a. What are to be the major underlying responsibilities of kings (or those in authority) according to Proverbs 16:10–15?

b. To what conclusions do these verses bring you concerning those in authority? Be specific.

Daily Discovery III **A Blessed Life (Proverbs 16:17–20)**

6. a. In Proverbs 16:17 what decision is necessary to stay on wisdom's highway?

b. What is the result of this decision?

c. In your present circumstances, can you think of any specific evil from which you need to depart? Obey God on that issue!

7. a. Name the two prerequisites to a blessed life found in Proverbs 16:20.

b. What will a woman who trusts the Lord be like according to Jeremiah 17:7–8?

c. Give illustrations of how you have found this to be true in your own life when you have trusted the Lord.

8. In Proverbs the word **life**, though used often, should be understood at different levels. Following are the various views of life in Proverbs:

Level 1: Life is described on a temporal, physical level in Proverbs 15:27 and 16:15. What gives you the clue to this in each verse?

Level 2: Life is the psychological or mental realm. What types of things encourage life in this realm according to Proverbs 3:21–22 and 14:30?

Level 3: Life has to do with the spirit or our relationship with God. According to Proverbs 8:34–35, what leads to spiritual life? In turn, to what does Proverbs 12:28 and 14:32 suggest this "life" leads?

9.   Show how the following verses in the New Testament elaborate on this same concept: John 10:10b, 1 John 5:11–12, and John 17:3. Do you have this kind of life? How do you know?

Daily Discovery IV **The Wise Person Speaks (Proverbs 16:21–33)**

10. a.   What will be characteristic of your speech when you are exercising a wise heart? See Proverbs 16:21, 23–24.

b.   According to Proverbs 16:21, how does the wise person "add persuasiveness (or learning) to his lips"? What type of "speech" do you think is being implied here? See also Proverbs 16:23–24 and consider how this relates to harshness or argument.

c.   In light of Proverbs 16:21, what specific decisions do you need to make?

Daily Discovery V **The Wise Person and Self-Control (Proverbs 16:32 and 25:28)**

11. By what strong contrast is the importance of self-control emphasized? Compare Proverbs

16:32 with Proverbs 25:28. In what ways could these graphic pictures help you explain to another the principle of self-control.

12. a.   Proverbs 16:32 reveals the surest way of attaining godly power and success. What is it?

b.   To what other conclusions do you come as you compare Proverbs 16:32 and Proverbs 25:28? State a specific way in which you could help another understand the principles here.

13. Name the areas of "control" emphasized in the following: Proverbs 16:32, 17:28, 29:11, and James 1:19–20.

Notes For Study Lesson 10:

_____

_____

_____

_____

_____

_____

_____

_____

_____

_____

_____

_____

Woman of Wisdom

Lesson 11

Friendships and Friends
(Proverbs 17)

Whether a society values the individual or the community, everyone longs for friendship. *Interaction, companionship, trusting,* and *closeness* are words used to describe elements of friendship. On the practical level, what is a friend? In the book of Proverbs the word for "friend" equally can mean "neighbor." This word, *neighbor*, has a wide range of meaning. At one end it suggests merely the other person, and at the other end it describes one with whom one is very close. In this lesson we will first examine that which destroys friendship, then look at the good neighbor, and finally consider the good friend.

Study Lesson 11

Daily Discovery I **Strife (Proverbs 17)**

1. a. Proverbs 17:1 could be called the theme verse of the chapter. What contrasts are presented there? Which side of the contrast most typifies your mealtimes? What part do you usually play?

b. In light of this verse, what do you think is displeasing to God within a household?

2. What can you find in Proverbs 17 that (1) might keep you from, or (2) might rid your home

of this displeasing element? Give references to those verses from which you make your discoveries.

3.   To what personal conclusions have you come in this matter? Take two insights from the verses above and show how they could be worked out in your home.

Daily Discovery II   **Help for a Friend (Proverbs 17)**

4.   Use Proverbs 17:22 and its further development in Proverbs 12:25, 15:13, 15, and 18:14 as if you were counseling a friend who was continually complaining.

5.   The word **repeats** in Proverbs 17:9 may not only indicate gossip, but also "dwelling on a matter." What is this proverb teaching us as wives or friends?

6.   a.   What is the other side of the principle found in Proverbs 17:13 according to 1 Peter 3:9?

b.   Give an example to illustrate each principle.

Daily Discovery III **and IV   Topical Study—Friends (Selected Proverbs)**

7.   Make a new heading, "The Friend," in your subject notebook. Set forth the "neighborly" qualities that please the Lord, and encourage friendship, as seen in Proverbs:

a. 3:29 and 25:8–9 (note the difference)
b. 3:27–28
c. 11:12
d. 12:26
e. 14:21
f. 21:10
g. 22:24–25
h. 24:17, 19
i. 25:18, 21–22
j. even in 6:1–5

8. Take three of the neighborly qualities above and describe a clear way in which you could demonstrate them to a neighbor.

9. Proverbs has specific things to say about:

What a good friend is	What a good friend is not
Proverbs 17:17	14:20
18:24	19:4, 6–7
25:17	25:20
27:6	26:18–19
27:17	27:14
28:23	29:5
27:9 (for example: 1 Samuel 23:15–16)	

10. Summarize the observations or decisions you have made about being a friend.

Daily Discovery V **Guarding Friendship (Selected Proverbs)**

11. In what way does Proverbs 2:17, 16:28,

and 17:9 indicate to you that even the closest friendship needs guarding?

12. How would you explain the statement "integrity of friendship depends much on spiritual resources" using the above references? Share your insights with someone else.

Notes For Study Lesson 11:

_____

_____

_____

_____

_____

_____

_____

_____

_____

_____

_____

_____

_____

_____

_____

_____

_____

_____

_____

Lesson 12

On Relationships with Others
(Proverbs 18 and 19)

In her book *Unfinished Business* feminist Maggie Scarf shares the results of her research in the causes of depression among women today. The author makes this summary of her research: "The core of female depression is the making and breaking of emotional bonds . . . . Both the career woman and the housewife are depressed not about position, power, or possessions but about unsatisfactory relationships with men, children, parents, and other women."

Long ago the living God revealed in His Word much concerning the basics of maintaining satisfying relationships. The biblical proverbs set forth many of these basics. But far from offering merely a practical approach to human relationships, Proverbs lifts these truths into the higher realm of ways to fear the Lord. The major thrust of this book teaches one how to revere God in the details of living. Therefore, as students of Proverbs you and I are to first make a decision to follow God's ways out of reverence for God, not because of a desire to have satisfying relationships. This decision, however, enables us to progressively become women of wisdom in the area of relationships.

Proverbs 18 and 19 help us understand how to please the Lord in our interactions with others. These chapters offer principles that can be applied in our relationships with our spouse, parents, and friends.

Study Lesson 12

Daily Discovery I **Being a Good Neighbor (Proverbs 18)**

1.   How can I be a good neighbor? List the answers Proverbs 18 gives, and check the ones relevant to you.

2.   a.   Write Proverbs 18:10 in your own words, using your name in the verse.

b.   What does this proverb mean to you:

- in your home?
- in difficulties?
- when you feel you have failed?

3.   a.   There is a striking similarity in the following two comparisons. What is it?

- Proverbs 18:22 with 8:35
- Proverbs 31:10 with 8:11

b.   What might be suggested through these comparisons?

c.   What types of wives are referred to in Proverbs 18:22? Examine Proverbs 14:1, 19:13–14, and 21:9, and explain what decision you need to make here.

Daily Discovery II **Gentleness Within Relationships (Proverbs 19)**

4.   Proverbs 19 indicates that gentleness and kindness are qualities of wisdom in all

relationships—marriage partners, parents, children, friends, employers. Discover verses that indicate specific ways to be gentle or kind as a

a. spouse
b. parent
c. child
d. friend
e. employer

5. By coupling Proverbs 19:18 and 19, how is kindness demonstrated by parents to their children?

6. In what ways can children demonstrate kindness toward their parents? See Proverbs 19:20, 26, 27.

7. How do the wise respond to others in general? See Proverbs 19:11.

8. In the following verses, what are you being warned against if you would be gentle and wise:

• Proverbs 19:2 (In what area of your life is this warning especially applicable?)
• Proverbs 19:5, 9, 28
• Proverbs 19:15, 24
• Proverbs 19:16, 29

Daily Discovery III **The Prudent Wife (Proverbs 19)**

9. According to Proverbs 19:14, how does a man get a **prudent** wife? What is a **prudent** wife? (Use a dictionary.)

10. a. Proverbs 31:10–31 expands the meaning of prudent found in 19:14 as well as elaborating upon Proverbs 12:4 and 18:22. Make a summary statement after reading these.

b. The following verses show the contrast by giving the opposite side of prudent. State the basic message of each verse.

(1) Proverbs 21:9
(2) Proverbs 21:19
(3) Proverbs 27:15

c. Define **quarrelsome**. Summarize your findings from the above passages, making your own comparison of the contentious and prudent wife.

Daily Discovery IV **Partiality (Proverbs 19)**

11. The hard reality of partiality that is seen in those not led by the Spirit of God is recorded in Proverbs 19:4, 6, 7. In contrast, God reveals His perspective and exposes the false values seen in these verses through the clear statements of Proverbs 19:1, 22 and 28:6. Summarize the contrast in these verses.

12. a. According to Proverbs 19:17, how does God desire believers to respond to the poor?

b. Using the following verses, summarize your understanding of what it is to be "kind to the poor," especially when the poor person is a fellow believer: Luke 6:38, 2 Corinthians 9:6–9, Matthew 10:42, 25:40, Hebrews 6:10.

Daily Discovery V **God's Plans Stand (Proverbs 19)**

13. Rewrite Proverbs 19:21 in your own words after reading Psalm 33:10–11 and Isaiah 14:26–27. What does this proverb now mean to you in terms of your own life?

14. Make personal (use your own name) the meaning of Proverbs 19:23. Try to include your understanding of what the fear of the Lord means.

Notes For Study Lesson 12:

_____

_____

_____

_____

_____

_____

_____

_____

_____

_____

_____

_____

_____

_____

_____

_____

Woman of Wisdom

Lesson 13

The Family
(Selected Proverbs)

"The Family is Dead!" trumpet today's headlines. Yet the family unit is lauded by counselors, psychologists, and social workers. Lead articles in popular magazines ask: "Can the fragmented family be pulled together?"

According to Scripture, God created families. God designed them to work best when each member reveres Him and His Word. In the Old Testament, the family unit was the pivotal point of society. In Proverbs this pivotal point takes on flesh and blood. Here we are given glimpses inside homes where parents act as one to faithfully instruct and rear their children. We view the practicality of households where each member learns to revere God in everyday life. And you and I learn how to please God through the daily experiences of home.

Study Lesson 13

Daily Discovery I **The Marriage Relationship (Selected Proverbs)**

1. In the Scriptures mutual respect and oneness is God's norm for the husband and wife relationship. In what area is their oneness particularly evident? See Proverbs 1:8–9 and 6:20.

2. God holds up marriage as the most intimate relationship of closest friends. Far from being

powerless and ineffective, the wife of Proverbs is shown to have a profound effect upon her husband. Explain the woman's role in each of these passages:

    a.   Proverbs 18:22 and 19:14

    b.   Proverbs 31:11, 23

    c.   Proverbs 12:4

3.   What is one of the significant factors upon which family stability depends according to Proverbs 14:1 and 31:10–31? What decisions do you need to make in light of this? Ask the Lord to enable you to be faithful to these decisions.

Daily Discovery II **To Love God in the Home (Selected Proverbs)**

4.   a.   Read Deuteronomy 6:5–7 and specify two key ways you demonstrate love for God.

    b.   According to Deuteronomy 6:5, what is to be the great priority of your life?

    c.   For the outworking of this priority in your home, list some practical ways you might implement Deuteronomy 6:6–7 in your life, in your home.

5.   Where do parents find the love, power, and wisdom to administer their special calling? See 2 Timothy 1:7.

Daily Discovery III **Parent-Child Relationships (Selected Proverbs)**

6.   According to the Scriptures, there are two aspects of parental instruction that are key for

parents to remember. The goal is to train, not punish. Yet correction is part of the learning process. Titus 2:4 indicates that mothers are to be instructed in the art of loving their children. According to Proverbs 13:24, what is one way we show love to our children?

7.   Look up the word **discipline** in a dictionary, then explain its meaning.

8.   After you have considered Proverbs 3:11–12 and Hebrews 12:6, state one way our Heavenly Father demonstrates His love for us.

9.   a.   Explain God's wise purpose for discipline found in

1.   Job 5:17
2.   Psalm 119:67, 71
3.   Hebrews 12:9–10

b.   Realizing that God is a loving Father, what do these verses lead you to conclude concerning the parental role?

Daily Discovery IV   **How To Discipline (Selected Proverbs)**

This section is presented from a parent's perspective, but there is instruction for all.

10. Why do you think God, who possesses all knowledge, as well as the ability to apply that knowledge to your child's life for their good,

•   used the word **train** instead of **teach** in Proverbs 22:6?

- used the word **love** instead of **hate** in respect to discipline in Proverbs 13:24?
- used the word **diligent** in Proverbs 13:24?
- encourages you in Lamentations 3:27 and Proverbs 22:6 to begin while your children are young?

11. What kind of "love" wants an easier way than discipline? See Proverbs 13:24.

12. a.   Why will the corrective aspect of discipline always be needed in training our children? See Proverbs 22:15.

b.   What is needed to help a child become wise? See Proverbs 22:15 and 29:15.

c.   From your own observations, give an illustration of the truth of Proverbs 29:15.

Results of Loving Discipline

13. a.   Name two things God promises parents in Proverbs 29:17 if they are diligent to correct their children.

b.   Can you give an example of this truth?

14. What does God promise as good results of loving discipline?
   a.   Deuteronomy 5:29
   b.   Proverbs 20:30
   c.   Proverbs 22:6
   d.   Proverbs 22:15
   e.   Proverbs 23:13–14
   f.   Proverbs 29:15

Daily Discovery V **The Warning!**
(Selected Proverbs)

15. Combining Proverbs 29:22 and Ephesians
4:31 with Proverbs 20:30, God makes clear that
our discipline is to be without _____.
Why? See Proverbs 14:17, 29.

16. a. What is the command of Colossians
3:21 and Ephesians 6:4?

    b. Reflecting on the key verb in each verse
what do you think this command means?

    c. Can you think of ways you might be
doing what this command warns against?

17. How might consistent discipline administered
in love deliver you from a nagging, destructive
attitude toward your child?

18. What will be the result if we do not heed
God's instruction? See Proverbs 29:15.

The Decision

19. a. What clear purpose did God have for
Abraham? See Genesis 18:19.

    b. Does God know this about you? Explain.

20. In light of this lesson, what new decisions
have you made? Be specific.

21. What is God's practical encouragement to
Christian mothers? See 1 Thessalonians 5:24.
Try to personalize your answer.

Notes For Study Lesson 13:

_____

_____

_____

_____

_____

_____

_____

_____

_____

_____

_____

_____

_____

_____

_____

_____

_____

_____

_____

_____

_____

_____

_____

_____

_____

Woman of Wisdom

Lesson 14

Decisions, Decisions
(Proverbs 20–22:16)

As we move line upon line, proverb upon proverb, through His instruction manual on the life of wisdom, God's gentle and persistent invitation follows us:

"Oh, that their hearts would be inclined to fear me and keep all my commands always, so that it might go well with them and their children forever!" (Deuteronomy 5:29).

The emphasis of Proverbs is to drive us to continual decision. What will I do with this truth; how can this be applied to my life? We are not allowed to remain hearers only; a wise woman is driven to make a decision to be a doer of His Word if her path is to shine "ever brighter till the full light of day" (Proverbs 4:18).

Study Lesson 14

Daily Discovery I **Man Needs Salvation (Proverbs 20)**

The general sinfulness of humankind with its resulting need of salvation is emphasized in Proverbs 20.

1. What facts concerning the sinfulness of people do you discover in Proverbs 20:4–14?

2.   Though our talk may sound religious, what uncovers our heart, according to Proverbs 20:11, Matthew 7:16–17, and James 2:14–17?

3.   Rewrite Proverbs 20:22 in your own words. As you consider Proverbs 20:22a, is there any situation in your life right now in which you are tempted to do this? In light of Proverbs 20:22b, what decision do you need to make? This is a specific way you can revere God; do it now!

4.   In the following verses, what actions keep us from sin?
    a.   Proverbs 20:7
    b.   Proverbs 20:11
    c.   Proverbs 20:15
    d.   Proverbs 20:18

5.   How does Proverbs 20:30 relate to the concept of sin? In a practical way, what does this suggest to you?

6.   One translation of Proverbs 20:28 reads: "Love and faithfulness keep a king safe; through love his throne is made secure." How might you apply the principle of this proverb to your life:
    a.   in the home
    b.   in an activity outside of the home

Daily Discovery II   **The Sovereignty of God (Proverbs 21)**

7.   a.   The sovereignty of God is the encouraging main theme of Proverbs 21. How is this theme conveyed in Proverbs 21:1, 31? (Note that the reality of God's sovereignty both introduces and concludes the chapter.)

b. In what ways do these verses encourage you?

8. As you read through Proverbs 21, make note of the verses that show you that God is in control of all things. Choose one and write out a personal application.

Daily Discovery III **Doing His Will (Proverbs 21)**

9. The other theme of Proverbs 21 results from the first. As we understand that God is sovereign, you and I are lead to do His will.

a. What is God's desire for us? Compare Proverbs 21:3 and 27 with 1 Samuel 15:22. Use your own name where appropriate.

b. Proverbs 21 gives some specifics of daily life, "acceptable sacrifices" we can offer to God. What are they? See Proverbs 21:3, 8, 15, 21, 29. Choose two and show a way to apply them this week.

c. What attitudes shown in Proverbs 21:4, 5, 7, 13, 17, 25, and 26 inhibit the acceptable sacrifices discussed above?

10. Give a positive or negative example of the wisdom of Proverbs 21:23.

Daily Discovery IV **A Prize of Worth (Proverbs 22:1–16)**

11. What is of great worth to you as shown in Proverbs 22:1? Why do you think this is true?

12. What do you discover in Proverbs 22:1–16 that indicates how to attain or maintain this prize of great worth?

Daily Discovery V **Danger Ahead (Proverbs 22:3)**

13. The principle found in Proverbs 22:3a is practical for daily life.

    a.   State the principle.

    b.   Where is the best hiding place from danger? The wise hide there (Psalm 91:1)! In practical terms, how do you think this is done? Ask the Lord to give you the opportunity this week to help another recognize this truth.

14. What two verses in Proverbs 22 give parents instruction that prepares the way for their children to have a good name? What are parents to do for their children?

Notes For Study Lesson 14:

_____

_____

_____

_____

_____

_____

_____

_____

_____

Lesson 15

The Counsel of the Wise
(Proverbs 22:17–24)

> "Pay attention and listen to the sayings of the wise; apply your heart to what I teach" Proverbs 22:17.

You have studied statements of truth describing wise and foolish living from Proverbs 10–22:16. You are in the process of discovering a way of living that leads to life in contrast to a way of living that leads to destruction. What is needed now is the challenge to put your learning into action. And that is exactly the thrust beginning in Proverbs 22:17 as the emphasis shifts to *application*. The appeal is made to "apply your heart" to what you have been learning; act upon your new knowledge. The emphasis is on our need to make a decision to do it.

"Make plans by seeking advice," Proverbs 20:18 states. Are you making plans? Seek advice!

The personal father-son appeals of chapters 1–9 return in Proverbs 22:17. Make this your prayer as you personally listen to the counsel of wise men (Proverbs 22:17–24:34). With their counsel, we enter a new section of the book of Proverbs—the Words of Wise Men.

Study Lesson 15

Daily Discovery I **The Words of Wise Men—Introduction (Proverbs 22:17–21)**

1.   a.   Proverbs 22:17–21 is the introduction to this section. What are the stated personal benefits to you in these proverbs?

Woman of Wisdom

b.   Which benefit encourages you most and why?

2.   According to the Bible, is it possible to know the truth? If so, how? Explain using Proverbs 22:20–21, John 8:32, 14:6 and 1 John 5:20. In light of this, what decision do you need to make?

Daily Discovery II   **The Words of the Wise (Proverbs 22:22–23:11)**

3.   a.   When God warns us about what to avoid, it is an issue of security and a matter of saving time. Study through Proverbs 22:22–23:11 and make a list of the things you are admonished to avoid. If it is stated in the proverb, note the reason the warning should be obeyed. (Deuteronomy 19:14 and Job 24:2 will help you understand the warning given in 22:28.) State which warning was especially applicable to your life and why.

b.   Now take four things a wise woman avoids. State the effect avoiding these things would have upon your home.

Daily Discovery III   **You, Apply! (Proverbs 23:12–32)**

4.   What are you told to "apply" in the appeal of Proverbs 23:12? (Hint: looking up the word "apply" might help you.) Give several specific ways to take action on this instruction.

5.   Realizing that your heavenly Father is speaking to you in Proverbs 23:15–16, what two things concerning you brings Him joy?

6.   What are you not to allow your heart to do, according to Proverbs 23:17? Why is this a waste of time? See Psalm 37:1–2, 23:17–18, and Proverbs 24:1, 2, 19, 20. How can you do this according to Proverbs 23:17 and 19.

7.   a.   In the midst of a culture that puts its heart's desire upon things material and temporal, what does Proverbs 23:23 encourage the woman of wisdom to "buy" and spend her time getting?

      b.   In light of our study in Proverbs so far, state a practical way you "buy" the above.

8.   a.   Several forms of self-indulgence are seen in Proverbs 23:13–35. What are they? What reason is given to show why each intemperance is ruinous? Give references.

      b.   In the midst of our temptation to indulgence, Proverbs 23:17 offers a safeguard so that we will not be overcome. Why might heeding this instruction be a safeguard from over-indulgence? Be specific!

Daily Discovery IV **Following God (Proverbs 24)**

9.   What do you see in Proverbs 24:3–7, 13, 14, 19, 20 that encourages you to choose to follow God's instructions, in spite of how difficult it appears or how much the wicked seem to be prospering at the time?

10.   Restate the meaning of Proverbs 24:10 in terms of your life. What can keep you from "faltering"? Let Hebrews 12:1–3 help you.

11. What practical encouragement do you find in Proverbs 24:16? What are we to do when we fall?

12. State the act that is displeasing to the Lord in Proverbs 24:17. When is this a particular temptation to you?

Daily Discovery V **More Words of the Wise Men (Proverbs 24:23–34)**

13. a.   What two foolish actions of Proverbs 24:23–24 are seen in sharp contrast to the wise actions of Proverbs 24:25–26?

   b.   In Proverbs 24:23–26, what are you being encouraged to do in your home and in your dealings with people?

   c.   Though a rebuke is often associated with harshness, how do the following proverbs suggest a rebuke may be given? See Proverbs 15:1, 16:21, and 16:24. Why might each of these approaches be effective?

14. Name two actions Proverbs 24:28–29 states you are not to do to your neighbor. (Your neighbor is anyone outside yourself, and usually describes those outside your home.) Do these verses indicate any exceptions?

15. a.   What main message is presented through the parable of Proverbs 24:30–34? What specific warning does this parable have for you?

   b.   In what way do you witness for or against Christ by how you perform your job in the home, neighborhood, church, school, work?

Notes For Study Lesson 15:

_____

_____

_____

_____

_____

_____

_____

_____

_____

_____

_____

_____

_____

_____

_____

_____

_____

_____

_____

_____

_____

_____

_____

Woman of Wisdom

Lesson 16

Wisdom's Reflection
(Proverbs 25)

Choosing to apply any one of the truths of Proverbs is to choose wisdom's path; to choose not to apply it is to choose against wisdom. This is as applicable for you and me today as it was several thousand years ago for King Hezekiah of Judah.

Two hundred fifty years after Solomon's death, King Hezekiah desired to go the way of wisdom. Thus, he led a revival in the land; "the service of the temple of the LORD was reestablished" (2 Chronicles 29:35). "There was great joy in Jerusalem, for since the days of Solomon, the son of David king of Israel there had been nothing like this in Jerusalem" (2 Chronicles 30:26). Because of his heart for God and God's ways, King Hezekiah became the greatest king since Solomon. King Hezekiah chose to be on wisdom's path!

One of King Hezekiah's godly acts was to commission a group of wise men to compile the proverbs of Solomon—now found in Proverbs 25–29—to encourage this people to know God's ways, to know the way of wisdom.

As you study chapters 25 through 27 in this lesson, you will note that most of the Proverbs in this section of Hezekiah's collection use comparison to teach truth. The figure of speech known as the *simile* is used repeatedly. A simile is a stated likeness between objects of different classes by the use of such words as *like* or *as*.

For you and me to understand these proverbs, as well as to have our eyes opened to areas of personal application, study alone is not enough. We would be wise to reflect and meditate upon Proverbs. Why? To reflect upon something means to consider carefully in the mind. To meditate is to dwell in thought upon a particular subject. Considering carefully and dwelling in thought upon a proverb with a heart's concern to apply it to life enables wisdom to take root in us. Instruction concerning wisdom's path becomes part of us. Then, in the daily issues of life, the wisdom of God affects our choices. A woman progressively cultivated wisdom as she makes decisions to apply God's Word. In light of this, it is interesting that the strong similes of this section stimulate within us a desire to both reflect and meditate upon the truths presented.

Study Lesson 16

Daily Discovery I **The Reflection Time (Proverbs 25)**

Integrating knowledge into life choices is a crucial step in the learning process. Therefore Bible study is incomplete until application is made.

1. What new truth, principle, perspective, or personal application did you get from the last lesson? What did you do about it?

2. Ask the Lord to open your eyes to insights especially applicable to your life as you read Proverbs 25. Jot down the verses that are meaningful to you and explain why. Make a decision to reflect on one of the proverbs.

Daily Discovery II **Hezekiah's Proverb Collection (Proverbs 25)**

3. a. After introducing the new collection in Proverbs 25:1, the first emphasis is placed upon wise leadership. According to Proverbs 25:2–5 what tasks are priority to those who lead wisely?

    b. How would you relate this passage to mothers?

4. The wise response to those in leadership is emphasized next. As you list these godly responses, state a specific situation in which you should apply each.

5. In what way does Jesus Christ emphasize the same counsel of Proverbs 25:6–7 in Luke 14:7–11? What do you think is the main concept of this counsel found in both the Old and New Testaments?

Daily Discovery III **Communication (Proverbs 25)**

6. Name the different kinds of verbal communications revealed in Proverbs 25:11–15, giving one reason why you think the simile that introduces each is appropriate. (Notice how the similes help you understand what God thinks of each type of communication.) Practice at least one this week.

7. What would you be doing if you were to apply the counsel concerning over-indulgence mentioned in Proverbs 25:16–17? Illustrate the

application of this principle from a real situation in your life.

8.   What do you learn about offering comfort from Proverbs 25:20? Ask the Lord now to help you remember this the next time you need to extend encouragement to another.

Daily Discovery IV **Response to an Enemy (Proverbs 25:21–22)**

9.   a.   Discover a way to overcome evil from Proverbs 25:21–22; compare that with Romans 12:20–21.

b.   What practical plan of action could you take in response to the advice of verses 21 and 22?

Daily Discovery V **Message Images (Proverbs 25:23–28)**

10. There's a treasure of challenging wisdom for your week in Proverbs 25:23–28. The graphic pictures that are used to illustrate each truth seem to plunge the truth into our hearts. Meditate on each truth with its accompanying picture. Choose two and explain how the pictures affect you.

Notes For Study Lesson 16:

_____

_____

_____

_____

Woman of Wisdom

Lesson 17

Wisdom's Picture Gallery
(Proverbs 26 and 27)

The portraits of individuals in Proverbs are often startling. Seeing them is like seeing ourselves on the museum wall! They show us what we are like, and we cringe and say, "Oh, I don't want to be like that!" This is exactly the effect the portraits are meant to produce! Proverbs' portraits of the Fool, the Braggart, the Bigot, the Arrogant, the Meddler, the Gossip, the Sluggard, and the Liar were meant to strike a jarring chord that we might *learn* and *turn*.

Study Lesson 17

Daily Discovery I **The Portraits**
(Proverbs 26)

1. a. In Proverbs 26:1–12 we get to know well the fool. Describe the fool using this passage as your source material. Note particularly the graphic pictures painted by the similes.

b. In light of the vivid picture drawn above, what strong point is being made in verse 12?
2. Put the portrait painted in 26:13–16 into contemporary terms, emphasizing the tragedy of verse 16.

3.   What type of person is portrayed in verse 17? How does the simile help you to better understand this person? What warning have you received here, and where do you need to apply it?

Daily Discovery II   **Destructive Conversation Illustrated (Proverbs 26:18–28)**

4.   What ironic truth is communicated through the picture in Proverbs 26:18–19?

5.   a.   Various types of destructive conversation are pictured in Proverbs 26:20–28. Summarize each along with any accompanying result. Choose one picture to discuss with a child or friend and record your insights here.

   b.   Explain the strong contrast vividly illustrated in 26:20–21 by stating which description you prefer to represent you and why. What decision do you need to make?

Daily Discovery III   **Boasting (Proverbs 27)**

6.   a.   Define **boasting** (a dictionary may help).

   b.   What two forms of boasting are mentioned in Proverbs 27:1–2?

   c.   The Scriptures tell us to boast, but in one area only. What is it? Jeremiah 9:23–24 and 1 Corinthians 1:31.

7.   What is characteristic of a healthy friendship? Describe how Proverbs 27:4–6 and 9–10 illustrate an outworking of Proverbs 27:17 that you've experienced in a small group or with a friend.

Daily Discovery IV **Powerful Pictures** (Proverbs 27)

8.   Read Proverbs 27:18 and then Proverbs 22:17–21 and 2 Timothy 2:6, 15. What do you think is the main message of these verses? In what area of your life do you need to apply this message?

9.   What insight does God give in Proverbs 27:19 to help you understand people better? Apply this principle to someone about whom you have had questions. To what conclusion do you come?

10. The restless frustration of our materialistic society is graphically portrayed in Proverbs 27:20. (Isaiah 5:14 and Habakkuk 2:5 also illustrate the picture in Proverbs 27:20.) How does John 4:13–14 and Philippians 4:11–13 help us deal with this frustration?

11. What do you think is meant in Proverbs 27:21?

Daily Discovery V **The Pasture Message** (Proverbs 27:23–27)

12. What do you think is the practical message portrayed through the country scene presented in Proverbs 27:23–27? Relate this message to your life.

Notes For Study Lesson 17:

_____

_____

_____

Lesson 18

A Matter of Obedience
(Proverbs 28 and 29)

We now enter God's priority program. In the closing chapters of Proverbs, various concepts are summarized into certain emphases that God doesn't want us to miss. Look for these!

Also, a very interesting thing happens in chapters 28 and 29. It is as if God considers that you and I, as students of wisdom, are now able to grasp the big picture of life. The approach to learning wisdom through parental instruction or the school teacher is left behind. Now wisdom is presented in a framework of life under God's rule. Directions of God are substituted for the authoritative instruction of the teacher. Parental education is replaced by the discipline of response to God. Isn't that what happens when we grow up?

Even prayer becomes an abomination if it is associated with inattention to God's commands. Thus one who fails to attend to God's law is a fool, even if he is a person of prayer (Proverbs 28:9).

Proverbs 28 begins boldly with a statement that reveals one of the great hindrances to the attainment of true wisdom: a frightened, timid conscience. The freedom and confidence that is produced by walking in the fear of the Lord with good conscience is contrasted with a fearful conscience that is continually fleeing when no one is pursuing! Circumstances that produce such a timid conscience are set forth in this chapter.

In Proverbs 29, the woman seeking wisdom is warned of the terrible danger of continually rejecting reproof (hardening her heart). At the same time she is given remedies for it. This lesson illustrates once again that faith involves all of life.

Study Lesson 18

Daily Discovery I **The Advantages of Righteousness (Proverbs 28)**

1.   What might be some of the reasons behind the truth found in Proverbs 28:1? (See also Proverbs 28:18.)

2.   What insight for our day can you get from Proverbs 28:2 after reading of the tragic cycle seen in 2 Kings 16:8–28 and 2 Kings 15:8–15?

   a.   What sad paradox is set forth in Proverbs 28:3?

   b.   Define **oppress** (a dictionary will help you).

   c.   What do the poor and the oppressor have in common? See Proverbs 29:13.

   d.   Can you think of any ways in which you might be oppressing others? (Proverbs 28:3, 8, 10, 15–17, 21, 24 may help you with specifics.)

   e.   If you have children, in what ways might you help them to not become oppressors?

3.   a.   Discover the two principles in Proverbs 28:4. Summarize the outworking of Proverbs 28:4a. (Romans 1:18–32 elaborates on this.)

b. In what ways does Romans 1:21, 28 help you to understand the truth of Proverbs 28:5, as well as the encouragement of Psalm 119:100 and John 7:17?

Daily Discovery II **Wise Family Living (Proverbs 28)**

4. Proverbs 28 offers useful counsel for a woman who desires to live wisely. Sum up the various aspects of this counsel in the following verses:
   a. Proverbs 28:4, 7, 9
   b. Proverbs 28:5
   c. Proverbs 28:25–26
   d. Proverbs 28:18, 20
   e. Proverbs 28:13, 24

5. If a child is to become wise, what should be the priority of the parent's training? If you're a parent, consider whether or not this is presently your priority?

6. Read Proverbs 28:10 along with Matthew 5:19, 18:15–17, and 23:15. Can you think of any way.
   a. you might be encouraging another into an evil way? (Try to be specific; thinking of your family may help.)
   b. you are encouraging another to do good?

Daily Discovery III **Danger of Not Facing Sin (Proverbs 28)**

7. According to Proverbs 28:13, Psalm 32:1–4, and 1 John 1:6–9, what happens to us when we

try to conceal our sins ? What will happen when we confess and forsake them?

8.   How does integrity or perversity develop in your life in light of Proverbs 28:14 and Proverbs 28:18? What then do these verses encourage you to do in daily circumstances?

9.   Put the practical theme of Proverbs 28:19 and 12:11 in your own words, inserting your name into the answer. Then ask some school-age children to tell you the meaning of this proverb as they see it. Record their insights.

10. If we choose to "get rich quick," what must we also realize according to Proverbs 28:20, 22 and 20:21?

11. As you seek to make application of the warning in Proverbs 28:21, can you think of any situation in which this proverb represents you?

Daily Discovery IV **The "Stiff-Necked" Person (Proverbs 29)**

12. The major theme of this chapter is dramatically summarized in Proverbs 29:1.

    a.   What do you think the Scripture means when it refers to one who is stiff-necked?

    b.   What warning is given in Proverbs 29:1 and elaborated in Proverbs 1:24–33 to motivate us not to be stiff-necked?

13. Read through the chapter and find five areas about which we are not to be stiff-necked.

14. a.   What guidelines does Proverbs 29 give for kings (or anyone in authority) who desire not to be stiff-necked? See Proverbs 29:2, 4, 12, 14, 18, 26.

b.   These same guidelines apply to you anytime you are in a leadership position (i.e., in a church- or school-related activity, in the community, at work). Choose one such activity and apply the above guidelines.

15. Summarize other guidelines for leadership found in
- Proverbs 14:35
- Proverbs 16:14–15
- Proverbs 19:6–12
- Proverbs 20:2, 5–8, 26, 28
- Proverbs 21:1–4
- Proverbs 23:1–5
- Proverbs 24:21–22
- Proverbs 25:2–7
- Proverbs 29:14
- Proverbs 30:31

Daily Discovery V   **The Snare (Proverbs 29:25–26)**

16. a.   Proverbs teaches us that the fear of God leads to life. In contrast, Proverbs 29:25–26 mentions a dangerous fear and its result. Explain by translating the Proverb into your own circumstances.

b.   Can you think of ways you fall victim to this fear? What solution is presented here? What then should you do in situations in which you experience this fear?

Lesson 18: A Matter of Obedience

Notes For Study Lesson 18:

_____

_____

_____

_____

_____

_____

_____

_____

_____

_____

_____

_____

_____

_____

_____

_____

_____

_____

_____

_____

_____

_____

_____

_____

Woman of Wisdom

Lesson 19

Woman of Wisdom
(Proverbs 30 and 31)

Remember the effect the study of Proverbs was to have on your life? The promise Proverbs held for attaining "wisdom and discipline; for understanding words of insight; for acquiring a disciplined and prudent life, doing what is right and just and fair . . ." (Proverbs 1:2–3)?

Exactly! That's what we wanted! But remember *how* these purposes were to be realized? "Accept my words and store up my commands within you, turning your ear to wisdom and applying your heart to understanding, and . . . call out for insight, and . . . cry aloud for understanding, and . . . look for it as for silver and search for it as for hidden treasures . . ." (Proverbs 2:1–4).

The result: "Then you will understand the fear of the LORD, and find the knowledge of God" (Proverbs 2:5).

We discovered the starting place for a woman who wanted to be wise. And the statement was clear: "The fear of the LORD is the beginning of knowledge" (Proverbs 1:7).

Though most of life's starting places are left behind, this theme, woven throughout the book, indicates that the starting place is also the ending place. Reverence for God is the foundation upon which true wisdom is built. At no point can there be wisdom apart from the reverence of the Lord.

But Proverbs is so practical. Proverbs 1 challenges us to "fear the LORD"! The rest of the book shows us how!

Chapters 1–9 set the stage to motivate us to want to know how. In these opening chapters, we discovered a father, most likely the editor of the book. This father was challenged to accept wisdom's path by his own father and now, knowing the blessing of this choice, he motivates his son to likewise choose the path of life. The father's approach in these chapters is positive—he is not so interested in all the "don'ts" as he is in showing his son the secret of being really alive and challenging him to cultivate his own love of wisdom: "Get wisdom, get understanding" (Proverbs 4:5). These chapters were designed to motivate the son (and in turn us) to choose the pathway of wisdom.

Then, in Proverbs 10 we entered the specifics of that path that "shines ever brighter till the full light of day" (Proverbs 4:18).

And so we proceeded through proverb after proverb that revealed how to live wisely. Through continual contrasts and comparisons between the good and the evil, the wise and the foolish, the righteous and the wicked, Proverbs has presented us with the paths of life and death.

In chapters 30 and 31 the style changes as the many proverbs are brought together and applied to your life and mine. How appropriate to summarize a book on how to live wisely by making application of the truths into real lives!

We move through Agur's personal testimony and observations into a wise mother's specific counsel to her ruler son, until we get to the climax of the book for us: the wise wife of Proverbs 31:10–31. In Proverbs 31 the reverence for God is the center and focus of both the ruler of the land and the woman in her family.

Study Lesson 19

Daily Discovery I **One Man's Personal Testimony (Proverbs 30)**

1. a. Read Proverbs 30:1–9. In a dictionary look up the word **humility**. Write out a definition for humility that has meaning for you.

b. According to the Scriptures, genuine humility is a sign of wisdom and greatness (Proverbs 22:4, Philippians 2). Thus, the humility expressed in Proverbs 30:1–9 demonstrates the writer's greatness. In what areas do you think Agur reflects humility in Proverbs 30:1–9?

2. a. As you consider these verses, what would you say has created genuine humility in the author? (Support your answer from the passage.)

b. What does 1 Corinthians 8:2 say about a man like Agur? What does it say about you?

c. If you have "played the fool and exalted yourself," what does Proverbs 30:32 state you should do? Practically, how do you do this?

3. a. Carefully consider Proverbs 30:5. What would you say is the purpose of God's Word?

b. What does the statement "he is a shield to those who take refuge in him" mean to you?

c. What present encouragement do you find in Proverbs 30:5?

Daily Discovery II **God's Creation Observed** (Proverbs 30:10–33)

4.   As you read through Proverbs 30:10–33, you will discover that the wise and humble Agur was also a careful observer of God's creation. Give a descriptive word or phrase to summarize each grouping of Agur's keen observations on life.

    a.   Proverbs 30:11–14
    b.   Proverbs 30:15–16
    c.   Proverbs 30:17
    d.   Proverbs 30:18–19
    e.   Proverbs 30:20–23
    f.   Proverbs 30:24–28
    g.   Proverbs 30:29–31

5.   In what ways are Agur's observations in Proverbs 30:10–33 an example of the worshipful statements in Psalm 143:5?

6.   a.   According to Proverbs 30:33, what will happen if we do not deal with anger?

    b.   Because of this, God has wisely commanded what specific action concerning anger?

Decision 1   Ephesians 4:26, 31, Colossians 3:8
Decision 2   Ephesians 4:32, Colossians 3:12–13

Daily Discovery III **A Wise Wife and Mother** (Proverbs 31:1–9)

The excellent wife of Proverbs 31:10–31 has been viewed as the summary of the book, demonstrating the application in a life of Proverb truths. Therefore there is much for all to learn and apply in this section.

7. a. What specific counsel does King Lemuel's mother give her son? See Proverbs 31:1–9.

    b. Realizing that the woman of Proverbs 31:1–9 is a mother, what does this passage imply about a mother's role?

    c. Make an application to your own life.

8. What phrase in Proverbs 31:10 indicates the value or preciousness of a wise wife? Explain how this passage relates to you.

9. What characterizes the actions and attitudes of a wise wife toward her husband? See Proverbs 31:11–12.

Daily Discovery IV **Proverbs Summarized (Proverbs 31:10–31)**

10. Let's see how Proverbs 31:10–31 summarizes the book . What qualities are suggested by the wife's actions in the domestic sphere (Proverbs 31:12–22) in the following verses? (Note that these same qualities were presented throughout the book.)
    a. Proverbs 31:12
    b. Proverbs 31:13
    c. Proverbs 31:14
    d. Proverbs 31:15
    e. Proverbs 31:16
    f. Proverbs 31:17
    g. Proverbs 31:18
    h. Proverbs 31:19
    i. Proverbs 31:20
    j. Proverbs 31:21
    k. Proverbs 31:22

11. What involvement does the wife of Proverbs 31:10–31 appear to have beyond the sphere of domestic life? See Proverbs 31:23–24. What does this suggest to you personally?

Daily Discovery V **The Key Decision (Proverbs 31:30)**

12. a. Proverbs 31:30 reveals the all-consuming principle that has become foundational in this woman's life. What decision has the woman of Proverbs 31 made that enabled the development of the above qualities? (Note also that this is the foundational principle of the whole of Proverbs expressed in Proverbs 1:7.)

b. Have you made this same decision? Why or why not? What changes would this decision make in your life? Be specific here.

13. According to Proverbs 31:30, reverence for God is superior to what two other aspects? Why? As a woman, what does this suggest to you concerning your priorities?

14. What are the stated results of the decision of life revealed in Proverbs 31:30? See Proverbs 31:25–26, 28–31.

15. Based on what you've learned in Proverbs 31:10–31, what changes in your home life or schedule do you feel you need to make? Explain. Be specific.

16. Do you see any relationship between the concepts in Proverbs 31:10–31, especially verses 10 and 25–30, and 1 Peter 3:3–5? If so, what?

So, you've begun! You wanted to be wise and now you know it's possible.

Proverbs challenged:
"Do you want to be wise? Then come."

Wisdom invited you to her banquet and you came. Now she asks you to stay.

"Listen to me; blessed are those who keep my ways. Listen to my instruction and be wise; do not ignore it. Blessed is the [woman] who listens to me, watching daily at my doors, waiting at my doorway. For whoever finds me finds life and receives favor from the LORD" (Proverbs 8:32–35).

Notes For Study Lesson 19:

_____

_____

_____

_____

_____

_____

_____

_____

_____

_____

_____

_____

_____

Subject Notes:

Woman of Wisdom

_____

_____

_____

_____

_____

_____

_____

_____

_____

_____

_____

_____

_____

_____

_____

_____

_____

_____

Note to the Reader

The publisher invites you to share your response
to the message of this book by writing Discovery
House Publishers, P. O. Box 3566, Grand Rapids,
MI 49501, U.S.A. or by calling 1-800-283-8333.
For information about other Discovery House
publications, contact us at the same address and
phone number.